RAFA
THE ROYAL AIR FORCES ASSOCIATION

Designed & Produced
by
Wilbek & Lewbar
90 Victoria Road, Devizes
Wiltshire, SN10 1EU

Collection by Rod Priddle
Editor Bob Wilson
Illustrations Ossie Jones
Design & Layout Emma Wilson

Printed in Great Britain

To Dame Vera Lynn
with warm regards
Bob Wilson

ISBN 1 901284 23 9

This book is dedicated to
Doug
Flying Officer D.H. Crosbie RCAF (J. 94650)
Observer - No. 575 Squadron

Foreword

Down the ages mankind has recorded the feats of heroes, great battles and the tragedies and miseries of war in poetry and song. From Homer's chronicle of the Trojan War and his tales of the subsequent wanderings of Odysseus, through Vergil and the sagas of the Norsemen to Shakespeare's great plays and the works of Göethe and Milton, down to the present day, men and women have been inspired to express their deepest feelings, their darkest thoughts, their hopes and fears in poetry.

It is indeed a tribute to the human spirit that the horrors, the slaughter and the sacrifice of the First World War should have yielded such a rich and evocative harvest of poetry from so many different hands. That tradition continued through the Second World War - and since, and has produced yet further riches, many recording that more recent dimension of conflict, war in the air.

This third Anthology, so carefully and thoughtfully put together by Rod Priddle, 'On a Wing and a Prayer' contains many of those gems, including another one by 'the Pilot Poet', Pilot Officer, John Gillespie Magee Jnr, who was so inspired during his days at Rugby by Rupert Brooke, also an old boy of that school. I have no doubt that all of you who read these poems will find them, as I do, evocative, sometimes deeply moving, like: 'Think Not That They Are Lonely' by Flight Lieutenant O.C. Chave. They transmit to us the feelings and thoughts of those, many long gone, whether laid to rest in some foreign graveyard or commemorated on the panels of the Air Forces Memorial at Runnymede, whose spirits look down from the lofty halls of Valhalla and, I am sure, nod as though to say: "Yes, those were our feelings; that was what it was like".

Foreword

When you buy this book, you are also helping to keep their memory alive through the work of The Royal Air Forces Association, caring for and providing welfare for those they left behind, their comrades and the whole of the Royal Air Force family - and we thank you most warmly for that.

Michael Stear.

Air Chief Marshal Sir Michael Stear, KCB, CBE, DL, MA, FRAeS
National President, Royal Air Forces Association
Royal Air Force Commissioner, Commonwealth War Graves Commission

Contents

Dedication	*Page 4*
Foreword	*Page 5*
Introduction	*Page 9*
Aircrew, 31st December 1942	*Page 10*
'Darky' Call	*Page 11*
Routine Flight, Mosquito, 1945	*Page 12*
For This Alone	*Page 14*
Fighter Pilot	*Page 16*
Dusk Take-Off, 1940	*Page 17*
Rear Gunner	*Page 18*
No Spotlight For Coastal	*Page 22*
Dedication Of The Memorial Stone	*Page 24*
Nine Days Leave	*Page 27*
Golden Caterpillar	*Page 30*
Old Airfield	*Page 32*
Air-Gunners Day At Runnymede	*Page 34*
Nesbyen Memorial	*Page 36*
US Eagle's Sacrifice	*Page 38*
Oh Once Again	*Page 40*
Think Not That They Are Lonely	*Page 41*
To Betty	*Page 42*
Flight From An Old Airfield	*Page 44*
Battle Stars	*Page 46*
Acknowledgments	*Page 49*
Other Illustrated Poetry Books	*Page 50*

Introduction

In my two previous books of Air Force poetry, **Wings of the Brave** and **Bombers Moon**, the poems had Fighter Command and Bomber Command as the main themes.

It seemed appropriate in **On a Wing and a Prayer**, to include works which pay tribute to other Commands and to the Women's Auxiliary Air Force. The airmen of America and the Commonwealth, who fought and paid such a high price to help safeguard our freedom, are also remembered.

My own collection of Air Force poetry has increased enormously since Wilbek & Lewbar had the courage to publish the first book for me in 1998. People have since sent me their own favourite poems or ones written by former colleagues, friends or family. I am really pleased to receive these. They have been added to my collection and may well be used in future editions.

Royalties from the sale of the two previous books have been donated to the Royal Air Force Benevolent Fund and on this occasion it has been decided to make a donation to the Royal Air Forces Association, which is also committed to the welfare of former Royal Air Force personnel.

Rod Priddle

Aircrew, 31st December 1942

Fighter trail etched white on blue,
Bomber captain, seaplane crew;
Like Gods; these men, though wrought as we
Are brushed with immortality.
Their youth not lost to age as years go by
But grandly, in a moment, soaring high
Through conquered sky.

31st December 1942
Lord Harold Harington Balfour of Inchrye PC, MC*
Parlimentary Under-Secretary of State for Air 1938-44

Major Balfour served with No.60 Sq. in France during 1916 after transferring from the King's Royal Rifle Company to the RFC. He returned to Martlesham Heath as a test pilot before going back to France in 1917 as a Flight Commander with No.43 Sq. In this role he destroyed 3 enemy aircraft plus 1 shared, and damaged 5 more. He left the RAF in 1926 and entered politics. He became Parliamentary Under-Secretary of State for Air having previously served as Minister of Aviation.

'Darky' Call

Through the static
Loud in my earphones
I heard your cry for aid.
Your scared boy's voice conveyed
Your fear and danger;
Ether-borne, my voice
Went out to you
As lost and in the dark you flew.
We tried so hard to help you boy
In your crippled plane -
I called again
But you did not hear.
You had crashed in flame
At the runway's end
With none to tend
You in your dying....

LACW Pip Beck - *WAAF 1941-46*

Pip Beck Joined the Women's Auxiliary Air Force in 1941 when she was 18 years old. Her first posting was to Waddington serving as an R/T Operator in Flying Control. During the two years at this station in No.5 Group she worked with No.44 (Rhodesia) Sq., No.207 Sq., No.420 (Snowy Owl) RCAF Sq., and No.9 Sq. This squadron moved to Bardney in April 1943 and Pip followed them there shortly afterwards. She went on to serve at No.16 OTU Upper Heyford and its satellite Barford St. John. Whilst at Upper Heyford she met Leo Brimson an RAF Wireless Operator /Mechanic whom she married after her demob in 1946. Pip has written of her Air Force experiences in a book A WAAF in Bomber Command published in 1989. This, and other poems she has written, appear in the book.

Routine Flight, Mosquito, 1945

Beastly chilly afternoon,
White and still.
O.K. be back soon.
Come on, Bill.
Blasted boots,
Parachutes.
O.K., Flight,
She's all right.

Good take-off from the 'drome,
With luck, you'll see,
We'll be home
In time for tea.
Nice warm Mess,
Wireless,
Toast and jam,
And - oh, damn!
Forgot to write
That card to Bet.
Have to get
It off to-night.

Now we're back.
Bill, can you - ?
Yes, there's Jack
Airborne, too.
Here we go
Swooping low,
With Jack
Some way back.
Under us pass
Downland grass,
Trees in clumps,
Houses in lumps

Like a kid's toy bricks,
Roads, bridges, streams,
Like you see 'em in dreams,
The whole bag of tricks.

Bloody fine plane to fly,
Makes you feel
You're riding high,
Half unreal,
But solid, too,
Safe and strong -
Hey, Jack, how long
Do we wait for you ?

Here we go.
At-a-girl!
Flying low -
Makes their hair curl.
Makes you feel good,
Climbing up steeply,
Diving down deeply,
Skimming a wood.
A splutter, a cough,
Both engines off.
Still in a dive.
Down to zero-five.
Diving still.
Makes you lose your breath.
My God! Sorry, Bill.
This is it.
This is death.

Rosemary Anne Sisson

For This Alone

Was it for this alone
we left the darkness of the womb,
the laughing childhood days?
To go
but children still
into the lofty places of the Gods.

To play
among the towering cumulus,
and flirt
along the pillared ramparts of the storm.
To watch great clouds
flower in ever-changing shapes.

And see
black crossed, sharp silhouettes
across our sights,
spin
flaming
down.

And then
to know the same fleet death.
The sweet sharp agony.
The searing change
from eager life
back to the shadowed mystery of Oblivion.

August 1942
Sergeant R.P.L. Mogg - *RAF No. 115 Sq.*

*Before the war, **Sgt. Mogg** was a journalist. He joined the RAF and served with No.115 Sq. at Marham in No.3 Group Bomber Command. On the evening of 30th September 1940 he was one of the crew of Wellington 1C, T2549 KO-K taking part in an operation to Berlin. The aircraft was shot down over Germany and P/O A.J. Steel and Sgt. Mogg were the only survivors. They were captured and it was in a German Prisoner-of-War Camp that Sgt. Mogg wrote this poem.*

Fighter Pilot

I know that it will come, but when or where?
In rattling burst or roaring sheet of flame,
In the green blanket sea choking for air,
Amid the bubbles transient as my name.

Sometimes a second's throw decides the game,
Winner takes all, and there is no replay,
Indifferent earth and sky breathe on the same,
I settle up my score and go my way.

The years I might have had I throw away,
They only lead to winter's lingering pain;
No tears call from those who perchance stay,
For Spring however spent comes not again.

When April brings more the gentle rain,
Mention my name in passing, if you must,
As one who accepted terms, slay or be slain,
And knew the bargain was both good and just.

Unknown

*These words were written by an American pilot serving at Debden
with the 334th Sq. 4th Fighter Group USAAF. The squadron
was flying Spitfire V's, with American markings, which they had
brought with them from the 'Eagle Squadrons'. These were
returned to the RAF after the 334th had converted to P-47
Thunderbolts in January 1943. The operations undertaken
were mainly escorts for the US 8th Air Force B-17's, with many
of the missions being deep into Germany and carried out with the
fighters using drop tanks. The sentiments expressed in the poem
were very much those felt by most of the pilots flying at that time.*

Dusk Take-Off, 1940

At the end of the runway
The WAAF corporal lingers,
Nervously threading
A scarf through her fingers.

Husband? or lover?
Or friend for a night?
Her face doesn't tell
In the dim evening light.

The Squadron is airborne,
But still the WAAF lingers,
Nervously threading
A scarf through her fingers.

Ronald A.M. Ransom

Rear Gunner

I feared for him.
His mind.
What he saw
hurtling backwards
to his private war.

He could spare only
a fleeting thought
for the enemy, in the city,
staring up, or hiding from the sound,
of a thousand Merlins
circling around.

When he glanced down
into the target's molten lead
incinerating the living,
or dead!
Suspended four miles high,
in fear and cold,
it was retaliation
he'd been told.

What words descriptive enough to tell,
of a comradeship in hell.
Or explain
what the torment was like
to have to come again, again.
Eight hours or more
is an age - on age!
With only a perspex capsule
for a stage.

As his friends,
torn asunder in the tortured air
to know only roundabout
the dank, grey clouds,
as shrouds!

On return to base
he couldn't grieve;
or a quiet moment spend,
or really quite believe
the absence of a particular friend.
From another crew
who only yesterday he knew,
In any case, it wasn't done.

There are no 'ops' tonight
an evening out instead
maybe only a twenty-four hour future
lies ahead.
Drink too many beers! Dance!
Find a girl! Laugh, Sing! - anything.
To hide that inner mind
already dead.

At times his face
told of a recent leave
normality to retrace.
Not this hideous make believe,
this stark, unreal contrast to home
where there was 'sameness'
nothing rearranged.
In the sudden quietness of his room
staring, dreadful at the papered wall

in his own bed curled
sheltered briefly from that other world
trying the everyday things to recall.

Down the lane,
the old stone school.
Village tea shops, bright awnings,
steadfast chapel, Boys'Brigade,
and breakfast on slow Sunday mornings.

The war took its course
he older, but young in years
still has no tears.
I feared for him more then
for what he saw, now lies
deep, unanswered in his eyes.

Some evenings in the village inn
at times, he hears the idle talk begin
and at the outside of the crowd
he quietly leaves
and has to be alone.
Hardly speaking, yet not proud
not feeling better than they
because he had hardly anything to say.
As he walks, his mind still wanders,
and in so many different ways
living in the memory
of their living days.

Flight Sergeant Ron Smith DFM, RAFVR
No. 156 (Pathfinder) Squadron

Ron Smith *joined the RAF in 1940 and initially served as a ground gunner. His operational service commenced with No.626 Squadron at RAF Wickenby followed by No.156 (Pathfinder) Squadron at RAF Warboys and Upwood. Most of his 65 operations were carried out with No.156 Squadron as a rear gunner on Lancaster 1's and 111's. In early 1945 he ceased operational flying and was posted to RAF Warboys, the Pathfinder Training Unit, where he undertook training duties. This involved flying with instructor crews on non-combatant circuits and cross-country exercises in a teaching capacity.*

No Spotlight For Coastal

'Bombers or Fighter?', his friends used to say,
But when he said 'Coastal', they turned half away.
Yet Coastal's patrols which traversed the Bay
Forced the U-boats to dive much of the day.

With the U-boats submerged for much of the day,
The convoys ploughed on, 'midst the salt and the spray
While the men on the ships did silently pray
That his plane would appear: both to circle and stay.

When his plane did appear; both to circle and stay
Then the Wolf Packs held back: wholly robbed of their prey
And the convoys sailed on in their purposeful way
And the seamen reached port where their loved ones did lay.

'Fighters or Bombers?', his friends used to ask,
'Coastal', he said, his face a tired mask,
Though not in the spotlight where others may bask,
We've a tough job to do and I'm proud of the task.

Squadron Leader Tony Spooner DSO,DFC,RAFVR
Flight Commander - No. 53 Sq.

Tony Spooner *is one of the well known Air Force officers to have served during World War 2 and is equally renowned as a successful aviation author following his post war career as a Captain with B.O.A.C. In 1941 he was flying Wellingtons with Coastal Command's No.221 Sq. based at Limavady in Northern Ireland. He completed a 'tour' hunting U-boats in the Atlantic. Following duty in Malta he returned to England for a training role with the Wellington equipped No.1 Torpedo Training Unit at Turnberry before becoming a Flight Commander with No.53 Sq. based at Beaulieu and St Eval, flying Liberators. A fuller description of Tony's military service appears in a previous collection of poems published as 'Wings of the Brave'.*

Dedication Of The Memorial Stone
At RAF Fiskerton 21st May 1995

Stranger - pause here a little while,
And listen to the West wind's sigh,
With its tale of long-gone men,
(Earth shall not see their like again).

Stand by this stone and lend an ear,
And I'll show you ghosts from yesteryear;
The windsock's creak, the cold wind's moan,
Long dead men crowd around - we're not alone.

Look on this empty, lonely place,
Unseen, do shadows still cross my face?
Listen! Far off thunder - or a Merlin's roar
Borne on the wind, from time's distant shore?

Abandoned, quiet, here I lie,
Time stands still, though years roll by;
Runways broken, dispersals gone,
The only sound, a skylarks song.

Half a hundred years have passed,
Half a century since I saw them last,
Lancasters, black against the sky,
Aircrews, young, so many soon to die.

They came from England and far foreign shores,
Volunteers, each one, to defend Liberty's just cause.
These runways know how many went,
Silent witnesses to Youth's blood spent.

I was created from the very earth from which they fought,
My rich, dark soil, with their sacrifice they bought;
In Lincoln Cathedral, yonder, their names are to be found,
And know this - by their blood, you stand on hallowed ground.

Let the tangled weeds that cover me remain,
Shrouding my memories of joy and pain;
And, as I return slowly to the land,
Let this proud stone in perpetual homage stand.

So, Stranger, continue now upon your way,
But forget not those who - it seems but yesterday -
Gave all their tomorrows that you might live,
For your Freedom, they gave all they had to give.

Cedric Keith St George Roberts - *May 1995*

This poem was composed by **Cedric Keith St George Roberts** in proud memory and thanks to those aircrew of both No.576 and No.49 Squadrons, who operated from RAF Fiskerton during WW2, from where his father flew as a Flight Engineer with No.576 Squadron. Cedric Roberts, who also served in the RAF, was voted an Honorary Flight Engineer for life by the surviving members of No.576 Squadron Association in Sydney, Australia on 25th April 1996 (Anzac Day). He is also an Associate Member of the Nos.103 / 576 Squadrons Association in the U.K. No.576 Squadron was formed from 'C' Flight of No.103 Squadron at Elsham Wolds in November 1943 flying Lancaster B1's and 111's with No.1 Group Bomber Command. The Squadron was transferred to RAF Fiskerton in October 1944 and remained there until the end of the War, finally disbanding in September 1945. A memorial to the personnel of the two Squadrons stands close to the remains of one of RAF Fiskerton's former runways.

Nine Days Leave

They ask you "What's it like to fly?"
And are you not afraid to die?
How's the flak? What do you think
Of when you come down in the drink?
They buy a round and shake your hand
Who say "I'll bet life is grand!
But not for me, I'll stay earthbound,
I'll keep both my feet on the gound."

How can they know, how can they feel
What in your heart, you know is real?
And how can you, with missing friends
Tell of that land where death impends
So impersonal, and yet so strong
Numbing minds, trips ten hours long
Where fate, chance - and so your friends
Hear that last mighty crash of drums.

The Reaper strikes, a dripping mass of flame
(The local paper prints another name)
Or fumbles at the door, just lifts the latch,
Then drops it, and moves away to snatch
Some other mortal, leaving you so soaked
With sweat when through the door you looked
And thought you saw yourself - standing within,
That life ebbed through your pores and blood ran thin.

You see six planes blow up, but they will be,
Just half a page in tomorrows casualties
Six sevens of men, each one will get a line,
Where before laughter, life divine,
For those who were not there, you only know
Quiet pity for a life they'll never know
Where life itself is sweet - but youth is past, and eyes
Can hide with smiles, what dread behind them lies.

That dread that comes to all in time,
That maybe you're soon to join those others,
Pete the baby, Binder Joe and Johnny, so you turn your head.
To look far off - to where their wounds have bled,
The wounds of chaps like Charlie, Tubby, Jake and Bing,
Their voices stilled that night above Berlin.
Those falling stars - down, down to a foreign land
Down, deep buried, and by a foreign hand.

Teddie, Bats and Dixie and Rollo and their crews
Old Pop and Tiny, Red, Mac - but what's the use?
You shrug your shoulders, can't say what you think,
And - not being God, "Lets have another drink."

8th May 1944
Flying Officer Cyril Keith Plunkett - *RAFVR No.619 Sq.*

F/O Plunkett *served with the RAFVR in No.619 Sq. No.5 Group Bomber Command at Dunholme Lodge. He was one of an eight man crew killed on the night of Monday 8th May 1944 when Lancaster 111, ND730 PG-0 crashed at Champigny-en-Beauce in the Loir-et-Cher region of France. They had taken off at 2151 hrs. for an operation against an ammunition dump at Salbris. Theirs was one of seven Lancasters lost on the raid. All of the crew were buried at Orleans Main Cemetery, Loiret, France.*

22 year old Cyril Keith Plunkett wrote this poem before taking off on what was to prove to be his last operation. After writing it, he screwed up the piece of paper and threw it into the waste paper basket. LACW A Stephen WAAF, later to become Mrs N Baird, retrieved the poem and has kept it to this day.

Golden Caterpillar

"Discard those overalls" the nation cry,
And "don this kit and learn to fly",
Soaring, climbing, looping, diving,
You'll become Masters of the sky.
Boys become men - the envy of others,
We're learning to kill our brothers.
Would they see us as we came on Wings
To bomb and bomb and bomb again?
Starlight above, darkness below,
Where is the purpose of all these things?

We had a rendezvous with death one Midnight -
O'er a flaming town.
Clouds scudding by beneath our plane
But moonlight broke through and brought a frown.
Would they see us as we came on Wings
To burn and blast and rage again?
Moonlight above, searchlights below, where's peace,
Goodwill and all those things?

"Attack!"- "Dive Down!" - "Going in now",
We always flew whatever the weather,
Knights of the sky - without suits of armour
But gauntlets of silk and cuirasses of leather.
Would they see us as we came on Wings,
To kill and maim, is this the glamour?
Aircraft above, target below, where's England
And April and all those things?

Too many times we courted Kismet
As we lorded o'er those skies,
With wings on fire and tail askew -
Falling through cotton wool cloud,
Smoke filled lungs, broken limbs,
Searching for parachutes through red-rimmed eyes.

They had seen us as we came on Wings
And we would not come again.
Victory above, success below,
What was the reward for all these things?
No 'Order of Merit', 'Jewelled Garter' or 'Slipper'.
Just a "Golden Caterpillar",

Sergeant Brian Burgess RAF Air Gunner - *No.214 Sq.*

Brian Burgess joined the RAF on 2nd June 1943, aged 18. On completion of training at No.4 Air Gunners School Morpeth, he joined No.214 Sq. in No.100 Group at Oulton and commenced his first 'Tour' in July 1944, flying Stirlings and Fortresses. He completed this on 3rd February 1945 and volunteered for a second, which he commenced twenty days later. No.214 Sq. were engaged in 'spoof' raids in support of the main force. 'Spoofs' were created either by electronic counter measures or the dropping of 'Window'. Brian took off on his 6th 'Op.' of the second 'Tour' on 14th March. Take off from Oulton was at 1720 hrs for 'Jostle' duties in support of an attack on the Wintershall synthetic oil refinery at Lutzkendorf. 'Jostle' was the code name for the huge 2,500 watts transmitter sealed in the bomb bay of the aircraft. The aircraft, a Fortress 111, HB802 BU-0 was shot down and the 10 man crew became P.O.W's in Stalag 7A. Brian escaped from the aircraft by parachute and wrote this poem whilst in the P.O.W. camp. He was released and repatriated on 25th May 1945 and promoted to Acting W/O the following day. He left the RAF in 1947.

Old Airfield

I lie here still beside the hill
Abandoned long to nature's will.
My buildings down, my people gone,
My only sounds, the wild bird song.

But my mighty birds will rise no more,
No more I hear the Merlin's roar
And never now my bosom feels
The pounding of their giant wheels.

From ageless hill their voices cast
Thunderous echoes of the past,
And still in lonely reverie
Their great dark wings sweep down to me.

Laughter, sorrow, hope and pain,
I shall never know these things again,
Emotions that I came to know
Of strange young men so long ago.

Who knows as evening shadows meet
Are they with me still, a phantom fleet?
And do my ghosts still stride unseen
Across my face so wide and green?

And in the future should structures tall
Bury me beyond recall,
I shall still remember them
My metal birds and long-dead men.

Now weeds grow high, obscure the sky,
0 remember me when you pass by,
For beneath this tangled leafy screen
I was your home, your friend, "Silksheen".

Walter Scott - *RAF Wireless Operator/Air-gunner - No.630 Squadron*

Walter Scott *served in the RAF from March 1941 until demobilisation at CFS Little Rissington on the 13th June 1946. The post of Wireless Operator / Air-gunner involved a lengthy period of training and so it was not until April 1944 that Walter commenced his operational duties with No.630 Squadron at RAF East Kirkby, flying Lancaster 1's & 111's. On the 21st / 22nd June 1944 he flew on the ill-fated raid to attack the synthetic oil plant at Wesseling. Out of the 133 Lancasters from Nos.5 and 1 Group, 37 were lost. 18 aircraft from No.57 Sq. and 19 from No.630 Sq. at East Kirkby were used with No.57 Sq. losing 6 aircraft and No.630 Squadron losing 5. One aircraft also crashed.*

'Old Airfield' was written in 1975 and has become very well known. It is synonymous with the former RAF base of East Kirkby. The words form part of the magnificent memorial which stands by the main entrance. It was recited by Nigel Collins in the BBC television programme 'The Watchtower' which featured the well known aviation author Squadron Leader Jack Currie DFC, himself a former Lancaster pilot with Nos.12 and 626 Squadrons.

Air-Gunner's Day At Runnymede

Each year we climb the winding road;
The bowery, emerald treed;
The long road, the ancient road
That leads to Runnymede.

And there among the lettered walls
Where those who seek may trace,
We feel, within, a quiet pride
In this our Island Race.

And those who came from lands afar
Who heard the nation's cry,
In death are now our kith and kin;
Their names will never die.

No known graves have these, my friends,
No sacred, hallowed ground,
But we remember year by year,
When springtime comes around.

And soon the spring will come once more,
And we will meet again;
For their most true memorial
Is in the hearts of men.

So let us then remember these
Of our proud nation's breed,
Whose names will live for evermore
In stone at Runnymede.

Victor Cavendish

Victor Cavendish *is the pseudonym of F/O Victor Cuttle RAF who flew with Bomber Command as a Wireless Operator / Air Gunner from 1942-44. He served initially with No.88 Sq. in No.2 Group, flying the American built twin engine Douglas Boston light day-bomber. In 1943 he joined No.106 Sq. in No.5 Group flying Lancaster heavy bombers. He was with No.83 (Pathfinder) Sq. in No.8 (PFF) Group, when on 25th August 1944 his Lancaster PB345 OL-Q was shot down on an unsuccessful operation to Darmstadt in Germany. F/O Cuttle, F/O Astley, F/O Scott and Sgt. Budd became P.O.W.'s. Sq. Ldr. Williams DFC, Sgt.Clay and Sgt. Gillespie perished and lie in Durnbach War Cemetery.*

Nesbyen Memorial

A bleak grave on the hillside, marked out in land unbless'd;
A plain unvarnished wooden cross; no names of those at rest;
Only a set of rusty nails, driven deep into the cross.
Tell how many died here and commemorate their loss.

This was where it ended for you - the pain, the fear,
Just one among so many of the tragedies of war;
And in that hour no witness, no timely friend was there
To hear your last words spoken, carry them to those who care.

But now your mission's story, the glory and the pride,
Is told to all your loved ones, unaware of how you died
And through the pall of sorrow that lies on those who mourn,
For sister, father, mother the bright memories return.

Rest in peace then, stranger, who for home and country's sake
Must sleep in foreign soil, never to awake.
The cold North wind shall whisper, over your lonely grave,
A final benediction for the life you freely gave.

Jorgen Syversrudengen
English translation by
Air Vice Marshal David Scott-Malden DSO, DFC*, RAF

Following an attack on the German battleship Tirpitz, anchored in Kaa Fjord in Northern Norway on the 15th September 1944, a No.617 Sq. Lancaster PB416 KC-Y, on its homeward flight from Russia two days later, crashed on a mountain top at Nesbyen, Northwest of Oslo. The aircraft was captained by Flying Officer Frank Levy, a 27 year old South African. He died with his crew and two other Flying Officers who were passengers.

The citizens of Nesbyen were forced, by German troops, to bury the men in a shallow mass grave close to the site of the crash. Shortly afterwards a wooden cross was put up beside the grave bearing ten nails, one for each of the airmen. A little later a poem was nailed to the cross by Jorgen Syversrudengen, one of the first men on the scene after the crash. He wrote it as a mark of respect for the men of a foreign country who were fighting for Norway's freedom.

When the war ended the Norwegians forced the Germans to bury the crew in the community churchyard. The graves have been tended regularly ever since.

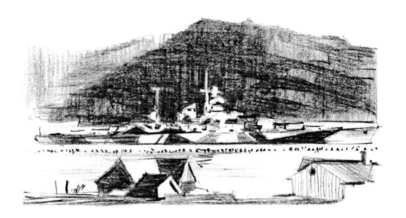

US Eagle's Sacrifice

Lord, hold them in thy mighty hand
Above the ocean and the land
Like wings of Eagles mounting high
Along the pathways of the sky.

Immortal is the name they bear
And high the honour that they share.
Until a thousand years have rolled,
Their deeds of valour shall be told.

In dark of night and light of day
God speed and bless them on their way.
And homeward safely guide each one
With glory gained and duty done.

Unknown

Some 240 young American airmen found their way to England during the early years of World War II and they formed Nos.71, 121, and 133 Squadrons of the RAF which became known as the "Eagle" Squadrons. The early arrivals to this country came mostly via Canada having crossed the U.S border in a somewhat clandestine operation as their actions were illegal in America. Not all came to our aid from a sense of loyalty to the 'Old Country'. They came for numerous personal reasons, many because of their desire to fly and the RAF's war time needs made it easier than the opportunities with the U.S.A.A.C. at home.

No.71 Squadron had been disbanded after WWI but was reformed at Church Fenton on the 19th September 1940. The first batch of 9 Hurricane 1's were delivered to the Squadron on the 7th November 1940 and following further acquisitions, the Squadron transferred to Kirton-in-Lindsey on the 23rd November and began operations. The second "Eagle" Squadron No.121 was formed on the 14th May 1941 at Kirton-in-Lindsey, replacing No.71 Squadron, which moved to Martlesham Heath on the 5th April. By this time there had been too many volunteers from the States to accommodate in one squadron. No.121, Squadron, like its predecessor, was flying with Hurricane 1's. The third "Eagle" Squadron No.133 was formed on the 1st August 1941 at Coltishall but, unlike the other two Squadrons, was equipped with the more advanced Hurricane 11B aircraft.

Oh Once Again

To climb aloft and watch the dawn ascend
Earth's haze-enshrouded rim. To dally high
And see the morning ghosts forsake their blend
For sundry silhouettes. To catch the sky
Transformed, its fawn and silv'ry tints now rife
With brilliant hues recast. To ease my craft
Below as golden darts give birth to life
And set the world astir. To catch a shaft
Of beaming warmth, and quickened by its touch
Assault its course through hills of airy fleece.
To burst at last above the crests and clutch
The fleeting freedom - endless blue, at peace.

1941
Pilot Officer John Gillespie Magee Jnr. *- RCAF*
Pilot - No.412 Sq.
(by kind permission of This England magazine)

John Magee is renowned for his emotive poem 'High Flight'
which is now probably recognised as being the most famous piece
of Air Force poetry in the world. He wrote it on the back of an
envelope whilst still under training at No.53 OTU Llandow. He
joined No.412 (Falcon) Sq. equipped with Spitfires at Digby in
September 1941. Tragically he had only been operational for three
months when he was killed on 11th December aged 19. His
Spitfire AD291 was involved in a mid-air collision with an
Airspeed Oxford from Cranwell and John Magee was too low for
his parachute to fully open. He was buried at the village church
of Scopwick near Digby. The headstone includes the first and last
lines from 'High Flight'. Although 'Oh Once Again' was written
in 1941 by John Magee, it is not known if he wrote it whilst still
in training or following his posting to No.412 Sq.

Think Not That They Are Lonely

Think not that they are lonely where they lie
Your tears are not the only ones to bless
Their sacrifice, for no one passes by
But pays his homage to their quietness.

As demi-gods they rest, and on each shrine
Are laid the votive gifts that children bring;
All Europe's flowers are heaped there for a sign
That their swift fame need fear no tarnishing.

Flight Lieutenant O.C. Chave RAF - *No.15 Sq.*

Flight Lieutenant Chave was based at Bourn in Cambridgeshire, a bomber station in No.3 Group. He was the pilot of a Stirling 1 BF448 LS-T which took off at 1825 hours on 14th February 1943 to bomb Cologne. His aircraft was shot down by a nightfighter (Ofw Fritz Schellwat, 5./NJG) and crashed at Helchteren (Limburg),14km north north east of Hasselt in Belgium. The eight man crew were buried on 17th February at St Truiden, though their graves are now at Heverlee War Cemetery. Flt. Lt. Chave was the son of Sir Benjamin Chave KBE and Lady Chave of Highfield, Southampton. In the Luftwaffe's recovery report, it is noted that two swastikas had been painted beneath the 'F' in the Stirling serial number.

To Betty

I'd like to show you England
When Mars has spent his power,
Show you all that England gained
In her darkest finest hour.

Hallowed monuments she lost.
Mars battered wood and stone,
And London was a flaming torch,
A sacrifice on freedom's throne.

Faith made that torch a beacon,
And free men were unafraid.
The sinews of war were flowing;
Sons and daughters came to her aid.

Come then as a tourist,
But see beyond her scars
The faith that made her whole again
And saved her soul from Mars.

I'd like to show you England,
The England that I know,
Of rain and fog and tweeds and tea,
A place where time is slow.

We'd walk the walls of Chester,
When the moon was a crescent knife.
We'd people old moors and castles
And bring your books to life.

And you would see why England,
Through quaint and devious ways,
Sustained the hopes of millions
In those darkest, finest days

June 1942
2nd Lieutenant Robert S Raymond DFC
USAAF Pilot No.44 (Rhodesia) Sq.

Robert Raymond *left Kansas City, Missouri and arrived in the United Kingdom to join the RAF in November 1940. His initial training was undertaken in this country before re-crossing the Atlantic in August 1941 for pilot training at SFTS Carberry, Manitoba. On gaining his 'Wings' he returned to England where, in January 1942 he served at No.2 SFTS Brize Norton before moving to No.25 OTU Finningley in March. He was working up on Wellingtons and when flying as 2nd Pilot on a routine daytime training flight in June 1942 he wrote the poem To Betty, whilst sitting in the rear turret. Betty was his girl friend back home and he posted it to her. On completion of training Robert and his crew were posted to No.44 Sq. at Waddington, commanded at the time by Wing Commander John Nettleton VC. Flt.Sgt. Raymond flew his first operation to Milan as 2nd Pilot on 26th October 1942 and completed his 'tour' with an operation to Spezia in Italy on 14th April 1943. By then he had been promoted to P/O. At the end of the following month he transferred from the RAF to the USAAF with the rank of 2nd Lt. He returned to America and served the rest of the war as an instructor with the US Technical Training Command flying B-17's and B-24's. He married Betty in December 1943 and was awarded the DFC at the British Embassy in Washington in March 1944.*

Flight From An Old Airfield

Bright morning sun, a sky of cyanine,
Head pillowed on a parachute I lie.
Deep in this long neglected, summer green,
Watching white cu. drift through half closed eyes.

Here once, a pale blue ensign caught the breeze
When long legged Stirlings flew the glory days.
The tumult of their thundering Hercules'
Rumbled across the fields and far away.

All's peaceful now, those desperate years long past
Where crumbling huts and quiet runways lie,
An empty hangar, rusting in the grass,
Deserted Nissens open to the sky.

The silent Watch Tower stares through shattered eyes
Its signal square now rank and overgrown,
No duty pilot scans the anxious skies,
Or friendly Pundit call the stragglers home.

So many winter rains and summer suns
Since they hauled down its flag and marched away.
Now long abandoned, overlooked, all duty done,
A part of England's history in decay.

Yet there are echoes on the wind that some will hear.
Faint voices singing half forgotten songs.
Young laughter drifting back across the years,
Long shadows of the old days lingering on.

Soon upward soaring larks I must outclimb
And, for a moment, glint in the summer sun.
As dauntless Stirlings did in that bloody time,
I'll too head north of east and soon be gone.

As my departing clamour ebbs away,
Silence will, once more wrap this quiet place.
Its ghosts can live again their gallant days
Of brave assault and resolute endeavour.

Flight Lieutenant Harry Loxton RAF - No. 2 FTS
RAF Keevil 1957

*Flt.Lt. **Harry Loxton** served as a flying instructor with No.2
Flying Training School, Hullavington in Wiltshire from 1954-57.
The subject is Keevil airfield in the same county. It was from
Keevil that the Stirlings of No.196 and No.299 Squadrons flew
on the Normandy landings and the Arnhem campaign during
1944. No.2 FTS used the airfield at Keevil as a Relief Landing
Ground from January 1955 to November 1957. With the close
proximity of Hullavington and Lyneham and the constant use of
the circuits at the time, it was decided to use Keevil for training
pupil pilots. There were occasions when they were billeted there
under canvas and their instructors would fly over each morning
with the Provost training aircraft. On one of these occasions,
during a quiet spell after his pupil had gone solo, Harry Loxton
directed his thought to the airfield's war time service and Flight
from an Old Airfield is his dedication.*

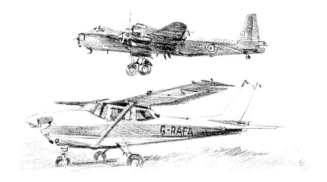

Battle Stars

Sitting alone in a cocktail lounge
sipping a cold mixed drink.
Thinking of buddies parched with thirst,
dead tired mid the battle stink.
Watching the debs and their playboy dates
drinking and having fun.
Wondering if even they knew of war,
or knowing, thinking it won.

A sweet young thing on the tipsy side
glanced up from her glass of Port;
And seeing the flyer alone and sad
figured to have some sport.
"Ah, look at the handsome flyer, girls,
I saw him first he's mine;
And look at the 'ducky' uniform
and all those ribbons fine".

"Tell me about yourself", she said,
"What do the ribbons mean?
What is the one up on the left,
and those stars - what do they mean?"
The flyer, embarrassed, and angered too,
got up and began to go;
But a sailor nearby said, "I'll tell her mate,
it's damn time she'd know".

"The ribbon itself is the E.T.O.
and each of the colors means,
The brown for the sand of the desert,
and the English fields, the green.
The black's the color of Germany,
and France is the white and red".

"The three stripes down the centre , Miss,
are all for the Yankee dead.
The stars, you asked what they are for,
I'll tell you what they mean.
They're four of the major engagements
and battles he has seen.
The Air Offensive Europe, the first,
but it means much more you see.
It's flak and fighters and comrades lost
early in forty-three".

"It's fighting your way to the target, Miss,
against all the Jerries that came,
It's watching your buddies shot from the sky,
going down in twisting flame.
The second's the Normandy Campaign, Miss,
it's the blood and slush D-Day.
It's the men we left on Omaha Beach
and the dead who paved the way".
"It's the broken and fallen seventeens
that burned in the fields of France.
They dropped their loads on the Jerry lines
and gave our troops a chance.
It's the LST's and LSD's
we left on the Channel floor.
It's the mines that burst and the bodies of
the first young kids ashore."

"The third one's for Northern France, my dear,
right up to the Siegfried Line.
It's paratroops on cruel barbed wire
and the filthy SS swine.
It's glider troops far behind the lines,
slaughtered without a chance.
It's the blood and guts of the infantry
spilled on the fields of France".

"It's burned out tanks and the slime and mud
and shrapnel and bursting shell.
It's mortar fire and the eighty-eight,
in short my dear, it's Hell.
The fourth bronze star's for Germany, Miss,
and the awful toll we paid
To cross the Rhine and the Siegfried Line,
and the lifeless men who stayed".

"It's the setback in the Belgium Bulge
and the kid next door who died.
It's the prison camps and the stinking food
and the filthy tricks they tried.
It's the land mine and the missing foot
and the man with the sightless eyes.
It's the brave young kid with his arm half gone
who smiles and smokes and dies."

"What are the stars you ask, my dear,
there on the field of green?
They're blood and guts and a hitch in Hell
that's exactly what they mean."

Stephen Quinn - *US 8th Air Force*
Navigator - 389th Bomb Group

Acknowledgments

I sincerely thank the following people who have helped me in the preparation of this anthology:

Wilbek & Lewbar for giving me the opportunity of releasing a new book in a new century and in the year which marks the 60th Anniversary of the Battle of Britain. ACM Sir Michael Stear KCB, CBE, MA, FRA&S, National President of the Royal Air Forces Association, for doing me the honour of contributing the Foreword. Ossie Jones who, with his illustrations, has accurately interpreted the theme of each poem. Bill Chorley for factual details taken from his series of reference books - **RAF Bomber Command Losses.** *Victor Selwyn of The Salamander Oasis Trust for approval to reproduce from one of their own anthologies, "Think Not That They Are Lonely".* **The 8th Air Force News** *for 'Battle Stars'. Kate Smith for her husband Ron's 'Rear Gunner'. Florence Burgess for her husband Brian's 'Golden Caterpillar'. Walter Scott for his haunting 'Old Airfield'. Air Vice Marshal David Scott-Malden DSO, DFC* for his translation of 'Nesbyen Memorial'. The publisher David & Charles for 'To Betty' from their 1977 publication* **A Yank in Bomber Command.** *Cedric Keith St George Roberts for his 'Dedication of the Memorial Stone at RAF Fiskerton'. This England Books for 'Oh Once Again' from their biography of the now famous John Magee,* **The Pilot's Poet.** *Victor Cuttle for his 'Air-Gunners' Day at Runnymede'. Tony Spooner, whose own books have given me so much pleasure, for his 'No Spotlight For Coastal'. Rosemary Anne Sisson, the popular film and television writer, dramatist and poet for her 'Routine Flight, Mosquito 1945'. Harry Loxton for his poem 'Flight from an Old Airfield', which was written on a sunny day while relaxing at Keevil Airfield, which nestles in quiet semi-retirement beneath the chalk hills of Westbury Wiltshire, of White Horse fame. Lady Balfour for permission to use Lord Balfour's 'Aircrew, 31st December 1942'. Pip Beck for her 'Darky Call', the type of message she was all too familiar with as a WAAF in war-time Flying Controls. To another former WAAF, Nan Baird for 'Nine Days Leave' by Keith Plunkett with whom she served. The Late R.A.M. Ransom for 'Dusk Take Off, 1940'.*

I have included some poems the authors of which are unknown and one by R.P.L. Mogg 'For This Alone'. I have tried without success to trace the authors. In the case of the latter, the publisher of his works has had no contact with him or his family for many years. I have taken the liberty of including those few poems which I enjoy reading and which I feel sure others will appreciate. I would be pleased to hear from any of the writers or their families in the hope that proper acknowledgement can be given in future copies.

Finally I would like to thank my wife Sue for proof reading the manuscript and my son Duncan, who in times of crisis has resolved my computer gremlins.